NIGHT PRAYER

A SERVICE FOR LATE EV

This service, freely based on the ancient office of Compline, can
be used to accompany an address, meditation or Bible study or
without an address as a late service with which to close the day. It
is suitable for use both in church and in less formal surroundings.

This is above all a service of quietness and reflection before rest
and is most effective when the ending is indeed an ending,
without additions, conversation, or noise.

NOTES

1   **Address**   If there is any address, instruction, meditation, or extended reading, it should precede this order.

2   **The Season**   This may be marked by the choice of hymn at section 6, an appropriate reading at section 8, and the addition of a seasonal collect at section 15. *Lent, Holy Week, Easter* provides psalms and readings appropriate to those seasons, and readings suitable for other occasions have been incorporated (see the Lectionary, pp. 18–19 below).

3   **Options within the Service**   The symbol ▶ indicates sections which are integral to the service and should not be omitted. Other material is optional.

4   **Saying and Singing**   Where rubrics indicate that a section is to be 'said', this must be understood to include 'or sung' and vice versa.

5   **Hymns**   A hymn is sung at section 6. If occasion requires, additional hymns may be sung at other points in the service.

6   **Traditional Texts**   Where parts of the service are sung to well known settings, the traditional words for which they are composed may be used. The Lord's Prayer (section 8) may be said in its modified form (as in Holy Communion Rite B) or in its traditional form (as in the Book of Common Prayer).

NIGHT PRAYER

▶ 1   Minister   The Lord almighty grant us a quiet night, and a
perfect end.

      All   **Amen.**

2   The minister may say one or more of the following.

Lord, you are in the midst of us, and we are called
by your name. Do not forsake us, O Lord our
God. *Jeremiah 14.9*

'Come to me, all who labour and are heavy
laden, and I will give you rest. Take my yoke
upon you, and learn from me; for I am gentle and
lowly in heart, and you will find rest for your
souls. For my yoke is easy, and my burden is
light.' *Matthew 11.28-end*

Be sober, be watchful. Your adversary the devil
prowls around like a roaring lion, seeking
someone to devour. Resist him, firm in your
faith. *1 Peter 5.8,9*

▶ 3   Minister   Let us reflect in silence on the day which is
ending, recalling our failures to love God and our
neighbour.

Silence is kept.

Let us confess our sins to almighty God.

▶ 4 **All** **Almighty God, our heavenly Father,**
we have sinned against you,
through our own fault,
in thought and word and deed,
and in what we have left undone.
For your Son our Lord Jesus Christ's sake,
forgive us all that is past;
and grant that we may serve you in newness
of life
to the glory of your name. Amen.

▶ 5 Minister The almighty and most merciful God
grant us pardon, absolution, and remission of all
our sins,
time for true repentance,
amendment of life,
and the grace and comfort of the Holy Spirit.
Amen.

▶ 6 THIS HYMN, or another suitable hymn, is sung.

To you before the end of day,
creator of the world, we pray:
in love unfailing hear our prayer,
enfold us in your watchful care.

Keep all disturbing dreams away,
and hold the evil foe at bay.
Repose untroubled let us find
for soul and body, heart and mind.

Almighty Father, this accord
through Jesus Christ, your Son, our Lord:
who reigns with you eternally
in your blest Spirit's unity.

► 7 One or more PSALMS are said.
If no special psalms are appointed, the following are suitable.
Each psalm or group of psalms ends with

> **Glory to the Father and | to the | Son:**
> **and | to the | Holy | Spirit;**
> **as it was in the be | ginning is | now:**
> **and shall be for | ever. | A | men.**

Psalm 4

1 Answer me when I call O | God of · my | righteousness:
    when I was hard-pressed you set me free
        be gracious to me | now and | hear my | prayer.

2 Sons of men   how long will you turn my | glory ·
        to my | shame:
    how long will you love what is worthless
        and | seek | after | lies?

3 Know that the Lord has shown me his | wonder·ful |
        kindness:
    when I call to the | Lord | he will | hear me.

4 Tremble and | do no | sin:
    commune with your own heart up | on your |
        bed · and be | still.

5 Offer the sacrifices | that are | right:
    and | put your | trust · in the | Lord.

6 There are many who say   'Who will | show us ·
        any | good?
    the light of your countenance O | Lord has | gone |
        from us.'

7 Yet you have given my | heart more | gladness:
    than they have when their corn | wine and |
        oil in | crease.

8 In peace I will lie | down and | sleep:
    for you alone Lord | make me | dwell in | safety.

Psalm 16.7-end

7 I will bless the Lord who has ⎪ given · me ⎪ counsel:
   at night also ⎪ he · has in ⎪ structed · my ⎪ heart.

8 I have set the Lord ⎪ always · be ⎪ fore me:
   he is at my right ⎪ hand · and I ⎪ shall not ⎪ fall.

9 Therefore my heart is glad and my ⎪ spirit · re ⎪ joices:
   my flesh ⎪ also · shall ⎪ rest se ⎪ cure.

10 For you will not give me over to the ⎪ power of ⎪ death:
   nor suffer your ⎪ faithful one · to ⎪ see the ⎪ Pit.

11 You will show me the ⎪ path of ⎪ life:
   in your presence is the fullness of joy * and from
      your right hand flow de ⎪ lights for ⎪ ever ⎪ more.

Psalm 17.1-8

1 Hear my just cause O Lord give ⎪ heed to · my ⎪ cry:
   listen to my prayer that ⎪ comes from · no ⎪ lying ⎪ lips.

2 Let judgement for me come ⎪ forth from · your ⎪ presence:
   and let your ⎪ eyes dis ⎪ cern the ⎪ right.

3 Though you search my heart   and visit me ⎪
      in the ⎪ night-time:
   though you try me by fire   you will ⎪ find no ⎪
      wicked · ness ⎪ in me.

4 My mouth does not transgress like the ⎪ mouth of ⎪ others:
   for I have ⎪ kept the ⎪ word of · your ⎪ lips.

5 My steps have held firm in the way of ⎪
      your com ⎪ mands:
   and my feet have not ⎪ stumbled ⎪ from your ⎪ paths.

6 I call upon you O God for you will ⎪ surely ⎪ answer:
   incline your ear to ⎪ me and ⎪ hear my ⎪ words.

7 Show me the wonders of your steadfast love
    O saviour of those who come to | you for | refuge:
  who by your right hand deliver them ‿
    from | those that · rise | up a | gainst them.

8 Keep me as the | apple · of your | eye:
  hide me under the | shadow | of your | wings.

Psalm 31.1-5

1 To you Lord have I | come for | shelter:
  let me | never · be | put to | shame.

2 O deliver me | in your | righteousness:
  incline your ear to me | and be | swift to | save me.

3 Be for me a rock of refuge   a fortress | to de | fend me:
  for you are my | high rock | and my | stronghold.

4 Lead me and guide me for your | name's | sake:
  bring me out of the net that they have secretly ‿
    laid for me ★ for | you | are my | strength.

5 Into your hands I com | mit my | spirit:
  you will redeem me | O Lord | God of | truth.

Psalm 91

1 He who dwells in the shelter of the | Most | High:
  who abides under the | shadow | of the · Al | mighty,

2 He will say to the Lord
    'You are my refuge | and my | stronghold:
  my | God in | whom I | trust.'

3 For he will deliver you from the | snare · of the | hunter:
  and | from the · de | stroying | curse.

4 He will cover you with his wings
    and you will be safe | under · his | feathers:
  his faithfulness will | be your | shield · and de | fence.

5 You shall not be afraid of any⏐terror · by⏐night:
   or of the⏐arrow · that⏐flies by⏐day,

6 Of the pestilence that walks a⏐bout in⏐darkness:
   or the⏐plague · that de⏐stroys at⏐noonday.

7 A thousand may fall beside you
      and ten thousand at your⏐right⏐hand:
   but⏐you it⏐shall not⏐touch;

8 Your own⏐eyes shall⏐see:
   and look on the re⏐ward⏐of the · un⏐godly.

9 The Lord him⏐self · is your⏐refuge:
   you have⏐made the · Most⏐High your⏐stronghold.

10 Therefore no⏐harm · will be⏐fall you:
    nor will any⏐scourge come⏐near your⏐tent.

11 For he will com⏐mand his⏐angels:
    to⏐keep you · in⏐all your⏐ways.

12 They will bear you⏐up · in their⏐hands:
    lest you dash your⏐foot a⏐gainst a⏐stone.

13 You will tread on the⏐lion · and the⏐adder:
    the young lion and the serpent
       you will⏐trample⏐under⏐foot.

14 'He has set his love upon me
       and therefore I⏐will de⏐liver him:
    I will lift him out of danger be⏐cause · he has⏐
       known my⏐name.

15 'When he calls upon me⏐I will⏐answer him:
    I will be with him in trouble
       I will⏐rescue him · and⏐bring him · to⏐honour.

16 'With long⏐life · I will⏐satisfy him:
    and⏐fill him · with⏐my sal⏐vation.'

Psalm 134

1 Come bless the Lord   all you ˈ servants · of the ˈ Lord:
    you that by night ˈ stand · in the ˈ house of · our ˈ God.

2 Lift up your hands toward the holy place ⌣
        and ˈ bless the ˈ Lord:
    may the Lord bless you from Zion
        the ˈ Lord who · made ˈ heaven · and ˈ earth.

Psalm 139.1-11,17-18

1 O Lord you have searched me ˈ out and ˈ known me:
    you know when I sit or when I stand
        you comprehend my ˈ thoughts ˈ long be ˈ fore.

2 You discern my path   and the places ˈ where I ˈ rest:
    you are ac ˈ quainted · with ˈ all my ˈ ways.

3 For there is not a ˈ word · on my ˈ tongue:
    but you Lord ˈ know it ˈ alto ˈ gether.

4 You have encompassed me be ˈ hind · and be ˈ fore:
    and have ˈ laid your ˈ hand up ˈ on me.

5 Such knowledge is too ˈ wonder · ful ˈ for me:
    so ˈ high · that I ˈ cannot · en ˈ dure it.

6 Where shall I ˈ go · from your ˈ spirit:
    or where shall I ˈ flee ˈ from your ˈ presence?

7 If I ascend into heaven ˈ you are ˈ there:
    if I make my bed in the grave ˈ you are ˈ there ˈ also.

8 If I spread out my wings to ˈ wards the ˈ morning:
    or dwell in the ˈ utter · most ˈ parts · of the ˈ sea,

9 Even there your ˈ hand shall ˈ lead me:
    and ˈ your right ˈ hand shall ˈ hold me.

10 If I say 'Surely the ˈ darkness · will ˈ cover me:
    and the ˈ night ˈ will en ˈ close me',

11 The darkness is no darkness with you
        but the night is as | clear · as the | day:
    the darkness and the | light are | both a | like.

17 How deep are your thoughts to | me O | God:
    and how | great | is the | sum of them!

18 Were I to count them
        they are more in number | than the | sand:
    were I to come to the | end · I would | still be |
    with you.

▶ 8 THE READING FROM SCRIPTURE
The passages printed below are suitable.

The Lectionary (pp. 18–19) provides psalms and readings for Lent, Holy Week and Easter, and readings suitable for other occasions.

At the end the reader may say

        This is the word of the Lord.
All   **Thanks be to God.**

Isaiah 26.3-5, 7-9 RSV

You keep him in perfect peace,
whose mind is stayed on you,
because he trusts in you.
Trust in the Lord for ever,
for the Lord God
is an everlasting rock.
For he has brought low
the inhabitants of the height,
the lofty city.
He lays it low, lays it low to the ground,
casts it to the dust.

The way of the righteous is level;
you make smooth the path of the righteous.
In the path of your judgements,
O Lord, we wait for you;
your memorial name
is the desire of our soul.
My soul yearns for you in the night,
my spirit within me earnestly seeks you.
For when your judgements are in the earth,
the inhabitants of the world learn righteousness.

Isaiah 35.8-10 RSV

A highway shall be there,
and it shall be called the Holy Way;
the unclean shall not pass over it,
and fools shall not err therein.
No lion shall be there,
nor shall any ravenous beast come up on it;
they shall not be found there,
but the redeemed shall walk there.
And the ransomed of the Lord shall return
and come to Zion with singing;
everlasting joy shall be upon their heads;
they shall obtain joy and gladness,
and sorrow and sighing shall flee away.

Jeremiah 31.33-34 NEB

But this is the covenant which I will make with Israel after
those days, says the Lord; I will set my law within them and
write it on their hearts; I will become their God and they shall
become my people. No longer need they teach one another
to know the Lord; all of them, high and low alike, shall know
me, says the Lord, for I will forgive their wrongdoing and
remember their sin no more.

Habakkuk 3.17-19 NEB

Although the fig-tree does not burgeon,
the vines bear no fruit,
the olive-crop fails,
the orchards yield no food,
the fold is bereft of its flock
and there are no cattle in the stalls,
yet I will exult in the Lord
and rejoice in the God of my deliverance.
The Lord God is my strength,
who makes my feet nimble as a hind's
and sets me to range the heights.

John 3.19-21 TEV

This is how the judgement works: the light has come into the
world, but people love the darkness rather than the light,
because their deeds are evil. Anyone who does evil things
hates the light and will not come to the light, because he does
not want his evil deeds to be shown up. But whoever does
what is true comes to the light in order that the light may
show that what he did was in obedience to God.

1 Corinthians 1.26-end TEV

Now remember what you were, my brothers, when God
called you. From the human point of view few of you were
wise or powerful or of high social standing. God purposely
chose what the world considers nonsense in order to shame
the wise, and he chose what the world considers weak in
order to shame the powerful. He chose what the world looks
down on and despises, and thinks is nothing, in order to
destroy what the world thinks is important. This means that
no one can boast in God's presence. But God has brought you
into union with Christ Jesus, and God has made Christ to be

our wisdom. By him we are put right with God; we become God's holy people and are set free. So then, as the scripture says, 'Whoever wants to boast must boast of what the Lord has done.'

1 Corinthians 2.10b-13 TEV

The Spirit searches everything, even the hidden depths of God's purposes. It is only a person's own spirit within him that knows all about him; in the same way, only God's Spirit knows all about God. We have not received this world's spirit; instead we have received the Spirit sent by God, so that we may know all that God has given us. So then, we do not speak in words taught by human wisdom, but in words taught by the Spirit, as we explain spiritual truths to those who have the Spirit.

Philippians 4.6-9 RSV

The Lord is at hand. Have no anxiety about anything, but in everything by prayer and supplication with thanksgiving let your requests be made known to God. And the peace of God, which passes all understanding, will keep your hearts and your minds in Christ Jesus.

Finally, brethren, whatever is true, whatever is honourable, whatever is just, whatever is pure, whatever is lovely, whatever is gracious, if there is any excellence, if there is anything worthy of praise, think about these things. What you have learned and received and heard and seen in me, do; and the God of peace will be with you.

▶ 9 **All**   **Preserve us, O Lord, while waking,**
                and guard us while sleeping,
                that awake we may watch with Christ,
                and asleep we may rest in peace.

From Easter Day to Pentecost **Alleluia!** may be added.

▶ 10   NUNC DIMITTIS is said or sung.

1 Lord now you let your servant | go in | peace:
   your | word has | been ful | filled.

2 My own eyes have | seen the · sal | vation:
   which you have prepared in the | sight of |
   every | people;

3 A light to re | veal you · to the | nations:
   and the | glory · of your | people | Israel.

Glory to the Father and | to the | Son:
   and | to the | Holy | Spirit;
as it was in the be | ginning is | now:
   and shall be for | ever. | A | men.

▶ 11 **All**   **Preserve us, O Lord, while waking,**
                and guard us while sleeping,
                that awake we may watch with Christ,
                and asleep we may rest in peace.

From Easter Day to Pentecost **Alleluia!** may be added.

PRAYERS

▶ 12   Lord, have mercy on us,
              Christ, have mercy on us.
              Lord, have mercy on us.

▶ 13   **Our Father in heaven,
              hallowed be your name,
              your kingdom come,
              your will be done,
              on earth as in heaven.
              Give us today our daily bread.
              Forgive us our sins
              as we forgive those who sin against us.
              Lead us not into temptation
              but deliver us from evil.**

              **For the kingdom, the power, and the glory
                  are yours
              now and for ever.   Amen.**

14   THESE VERSICLES AND RESPONSES may be said.

Minister   We will lie down in peace, and take our rest;
All   **for you alone, Lord, make us dwell in
                  safety.**

Minister   Into your hands, O Lord, I commit my spirit;
All   **you will redeem me, O Lord God of truth.**

Minister   Keep us tonight, Lord, from all sin;
All   **have mercy on us, Lord, have mercy.**

Minister   Lord, hear our prayer;
All   **and let our cry come to you.**

15   One or more of these COLLECTS may be said.

Visit, Lord, we pray, this place,
and drive far from it all the snares of evil.
Let your holy angels dwell here to keep us
    in peace,
and may your blessing be upon us evermore;
through Jesus Christ our Lord.   **Amen.**

Lighten our darkness, Lord, we pray;
and in your mercy defend us
from all perils and dangers of this night;
for the love of your only Son,
our Saviour Jesus Christ.   **Amen.**

Be with us, merciful God,
and protect us through the silent hours of
    this night,
so that we, who are wearied
by the changes and chances of this fleeting world,
may rest upon your eternal changelessness;
through Jesus Christ our Lord.   **Amen.**

Look down, Lord, from your heavenly throne;
lighten the darkness of the night
with your celestial brightness;
and from the children of light
banish the deeds of darkness;
through Jesus Christ our Lord.   **Amen.**

Lord Jesus Christ,
Son of the living God,
who at this evening hour rested in the sepulchre,
and sanctified the grave
to be a bed of hope to your people:
make us so deeply sorry for our sins,
which were the cause of your passion,

that when our bodies lie in the dust,
our souls may live with you;
for with the Father and the Holy Spirit
you live and reign, now and for ever.   **Amen.**

THIS COLLECT is appropriate on Sundays and from Easter
Day to Pentecost.

O Lord,
who by triumphing over the power of darkness
prepared our place in the new Jerusalem:
grant that we, who have this day
    given thanks for your resurrection,
may praise you in the city where you are
    the light;
for there with the Father and the Holy Spirit
you live and reign, now and for ever.   **Amen.**

▶ 16   Minister   The Lord be with you
       All   **and also with you.**

  17   Minister   Let us bless the Lord.
       All   **Thanks be to God.**

From Easter Day to Pentecost **Alleluia! Alleluia!** may be
added after both the versicle and the response.

▶ 18   Minister   The almighty and merciful Lord,
                   Father, Son, and Holy Spirit,
                   bless us and keep us, this night and for evermore.
       All   **Amen.**

A LECTIONARY FOR NIGHT PRAYER

from *Lent, Holy Week, Easter*

The options marked A, B and C extend over Morning Prayer, the Holy Communion, Evening Prayer and Night Prayer and should be used consistently in any one year.

	Psalms	Readings
Ash Wednesday	90	Ezek 18. 21–22, 30b–end
Palm Sunday	55	Zech 12.8, 10
Monday in Holy Week	71	A Heb 2. 9–end
		B Heb 2.9–end
		C Gal 6.11–end
Tuesday in Holy Week	73	A Heb 8. 1–6
		B Heb 8. 1–6
		C Eph 2. 11–18
Wednesday in Holy Week	102	A Phil 3. 7–11
		B Phil 3. 7–11
		C 1 Cor 1. 18–25
Maundy Thursday	54	A Luke 22. 31–65
		B Matt 26. 30–end
		C Mark 14. 26–end
Good Friday	140. 1–8, 12–end	A Luke 23. 50–end
		B Matt 27. 55–61
		C Mark 15. 40–end
		or Col 1. 15–23
Easter Eve	30	Phil 2. 5–11
Easter Day	115	1 Cor 5. 6–8
Monday in Easter Week	2	Rom 8. 9–11
Tuesday in Easter Week	23	Heb 13. 20–21
Wednesday in Easter Week	93	2 Cor 5. 14–17
Thursday in Easter Week	111	Eph 2. 4–10
Friday in Easter Week	113	Rom 14. 7–9
Saturday in Easter Week	16	1 Cor 15. 20–22
First Sunday after Easter	48	2 Tim 1. 8–10
Ascension Eve	98	Heb 10. 12–14
Ascension Day	8	Eph 2. 4–10
Sunday after Ascension	146	Phil 2. 5–11
Pentecost Eve	143. 1–11	Isa 11. 1–3
Pentecost	48	2 Cor 1. 21–22

Readings Suitable for Other Occasions

Advent	Isaiah 45. 5–8
	Mark 13. 35–end
	1 Corinthians 4. 3–5
	Philippians 3. 20–end
	1 Thessalonians 3. 12–end
	1 Thessalonians 5. 23–24
Christmas, Presentation, Annunciation	Wisdom 18. 14–15a
	John 1. 4–5
	John 1. 14–18
	1 John 1. 1–3
Epiphany	Isaiah 9. 2, 6–7
	Isaiah 61. 1–3
	Tobit 13. 11
	2 Timothy 1. 9–10
	Titus 2. 11–13
	Revelation 21. 23–24
Lent	Ephesians 4. 26–27
	1 Thessalonians 5. 9–10
	1 Peter 5. 6–7
After Pentecost	Deuteronomy 6. 4–7
	Isaiah 30. 15
	John 14. 26–27
Dedication	Haggai 2. 6–9
St Joseph, Blessed Virgin Mary	Isaiah 7. 14–15
	Galatians 4. 4–7
St John Baptist	1 Peter 1. 8–12
Saints' Days	Ephesians 1. 15–18
	Hebrews 12. 22–24
	Revelation 22. 4–5

ACKNOWLEDGEMENTS

Biblical passages are reproduced with permission from

The Revised Standard Version of the Bible (RSV), copyright 1946, 1952, © 1971, 1973 by The Division of Christian Education of the National Council of the Churches of Christ in the USA

The New English Bible (NEB), © 1961, 1970 Oxford and Cambridge University Presses

Today's English Version (TEV), © American Bible Society 1966, 1971, 1976. British usage edition *Good News Bible* published 1976 by The Bible Societies and Collins

Psalms printed within the service follow the text and pointing of the Liturgical Psalter first published as *The Psalms: a new translation for worship,* © English text 1976, 1977, David L Frost, John A Emerton, Andrew A Macintosh, all rights reserved, © pointing 1976, 1977 William Collins Sons & Co Ltd

Those who prepared this service wish to record their indebtedness to *The Office of Compline – An Alternative Order,* © David Silk 1980 (Mowbray)

Church House Publishing
Church House, Great Smith Street, London SW1P 3NZ

ISBN 0 7151 3713 1

Set in Monophoto Bembo by Servis Filmsetting Ltd, Manchester
Printed in Great Britain by Martin's the Printers Ltd, Berwick upon Tweed